Pears
PUBLISI
D0589245

Technical Companion to Drama

Brian McGuire

Brian McGuire is the head of a large Expressive Arts faculty. He has a great deal of experience as a senior examiner for drama. He is recognised as one of the country's leading authorities on drama.

Illustrations by Gary Hogg

Acknowledgement

The author is grateful to the following students for the example extracts which are based on their work: Kirsty Jolly, Laura Hart, Sarah Ellison, Katie Barrett, Clara Connelly, Leeanne Stacey, Emma Stockton, David Bracewell, Debra Jones and John Smith.

Name ....

Address ....

....

....

Exam board ....

Syllabus number ....

Candidate number ....

Centre number ....

Coursework deadlines ....

....

Examination dates ....

....

....

Further copies of this publication may be obtained from:

Pearson Publishing
Chesterton Mill, French's Road, Cambridge CB4 3NP
Tel 01223 350555   Fax 01223 356484

Email info@pearson.co.uk   Web site www.pearsonpublishing.co.uk

ISBN: 1 85749 627 2

Published by Pearson Publishing 2000
© Pearson Publishing 2000
First reprint 2001

Contents

Introduction

The aim of this handbook is to explain some of the technical aspects of drama you would use during drama lessons, practical drama examinations, workshop presentations and school productions. Sections 1 to 6 of the book concentrate on:

- lighting
- sound
- costume
- properties
- set design
- stage management.

These sections give you information about equipment you might use and responsibilities you may undertake. They also provide example cue sheets, blank cue sheets and worksheets for you to complete.

The book is also meant to be a companion to the *Student Handbook for Drama*, available from Pearson Publishing. Hence, the following are included:

- further performance tips
- more drama techniques your teacher may use
- notes on writing scripts, information on performing rights and more examples of written work.

It is suitable for KS3, GCSE, A-level and GNVQ Drama and Performing Arts courses.

1 Lighting

*"But, soft! what light through
yonder window breaks?"*

(Romeo and Juliet)

Drama studios, halls, theatres, etc have specialist lights. These are called lanterns. They have two main purposes:

- to focus our vision on a particular part or on all of the acting area
- to create atmosphere.

The basic rule is: Better too much light than not enough.

Fading in/out

Often, the lighting engineer will fade in the lights. As this occurs, for a brief moment, the audience can see the actors in position ready to start. Here is an opportunity to create an effective visual image. The start of a piece of drama is very important – it sets the tone for what will follow. This moment is worth spending time on.

Sometimes a fade in may last up to 45 seconds. Begin the action, or speak as soon as there is sufficient light on the acting area for the audience to see. Once the lights start to intensify, don't wait for them to be fully lit. Often, students wait too long before starting their drama.

Just as the moment you may hold at the beginning of the fade in is important, then the end of the scene is equally important. You should always try to create an effective image, especially if the lights are going to fade out slowly, thus leaving the audience thinking about the final picture of the drama.

Lighting without lanterns

As well as using the lanterns to create particular visual effects, there are other popular ways of creating atmosphere. The use of a lighted candle held by the actor near the face gives an interesting dramatic effect. Often when candles are used, it is necessary to add a little light from the lanterns.

There are, however, possible problems with using candles. When striking matches to light the candle, the matches may break, it may need several strikes to light the match or it may take a while for the candle to light. In your drama, it is essential that you do not lose time because of small technical problems. If you use lighted candles, then there is always the risk of fire so don't forget to discuss it with your teacher first.

Shining a torch onto the actor's face also gives an interesting dramatic effect. A common technique is for the actors to hold a small torch at their chin and shine it upwards.

The actor can also shine the torch onto another actor's face. Always check the batteries are working.

Finding your light

Certain parts of the acting area will be lit more than others. Sometimes it is necessary to 'find your light'. This means moving to the area onstage that is appropriately lit. An example might be that in one area there is a spotlight that you need to move into when you are going to sing a song. Maybe the spotlight is coloured so that as you step into that area the atmosphere changes. Actors need to be aware of where they should be standing in relation to the lanterns. Sometimes, a director will mark a particular spot with chalk marks to get the actors used to finding the space where they should be.

Houselights

These are the ordinary lights in the auditorium or drama studio. Before the presentation of a piece of work, try to take the houselights out by dimming them. It helps to create an atmosphere of anticipation. Houselights may be on a dimmer. If they are not, then turn off the light switches one at a time, turning off the lights furthest away from the acting area first.

The lanterns

Light bulbs in your house are generally 60-100 watts. Bulbs used in lanterns are 500-1000 watts and sometimes stronger. These bulbs are very expensive and great care must be taken not to knock the lantern or bulb. The lanterns fall into three categories, although there are variations within each:

- the profile spotlight
- the fresnel spotlight
- the flood.

The profile spotlight
The profile spotlight creates a hard edge to the circle of light.

The fresnel spotlight

The fresnel spotlight lights a particular area but the edge is soft, not hard.

The flood

Floods give general light. They flood the acting area with light. Like other lanterns, they will hang from the lighting bar and can be shone from various angles.

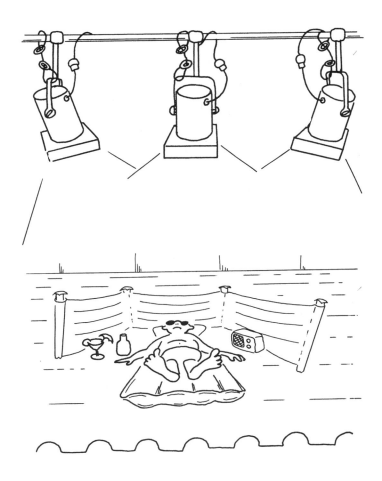

Safety chain and 'G' clamp

As well as a clamp (usually called a 'G' clamp) to secure the lantern to the lighting bar, each lantern should have a safety chain. The chain links through the lantern support and round the lighting bar.

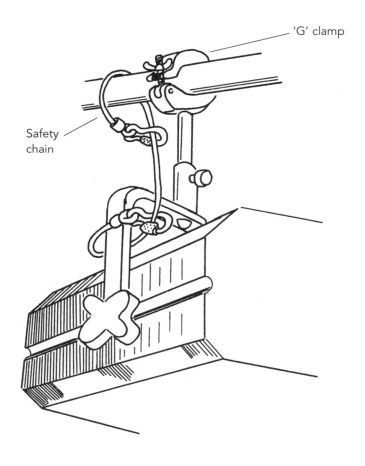

'G' clamp

Safety chain

Never hang a lantern without a safety chain!

Barn doors

Barn doors are four metal hinged flaps on a small frame that slots into the front of the lantern. They can be opened or closed to help control or shape the beam from the lantern. They stop the light spilling out and focus it on a particular area.

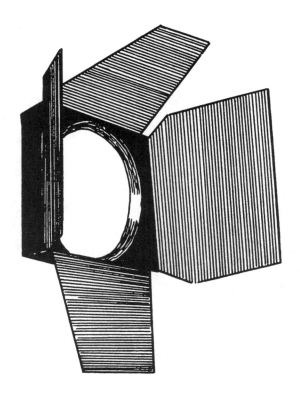

Using colour (cinemoid)

Creating atmosphere through the use of colour is done by using cinemoid. There is a bracket at the front of the spotlight into which the cinemoid holder can be inserted.

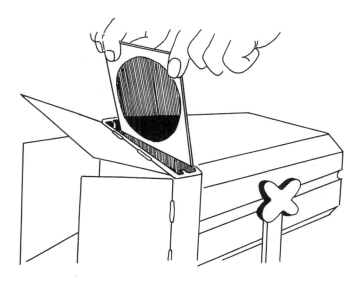

Cinemoid comes in many different colours but you must remember that it is expensive. The colours can be symbolic. For example, the stage can be flooded in red to symbolise danger. Green can be shone on witches, etc. Costume and set colours will be enhanced by coloured cinemoid. For example, if the set contains lots of plants, trees, etc, green cinemoid will help the effect. If you are creating a piece for examinations, then try to use colour to help the effect. Remember that your teacher may be organising the lighting for a number of groups so the earlier you know what you want, the more chance you have of getting it.

Gobos

Gobos are metal cut-outs which can be placed at the front of the spotlight. They are used to create effects. For example, the cut-out can be in the shape of a star. Cut-out lines can create the effect of prison. This is an effective and cheap way of creating a set.

Strobe lighting

Strobe lighting gives the effect of slowing down the action. It can be very effective in fight scenes, scenes of disasters or frantic action. However, if ever strobe lighting is used, the audience should be informed beforehand. The information should be in the programme and advertised in the auditorium. Strobe lighting can induce epileptic fits so it should be used sparingly.

Cyclorama

The cyclorama is the large screen upstage onto which images or the lanterns can be projected. At a simple level, colour can be projected through the lanterns and used to represent place, for example, red for one place and green for another. If the set is the seaside, then a light blue can be projected onto the cyclorama as a complimentary colour to the staging area which may be painted yellow.

Lighting the actor

If the actor is only lit from one side, then a shadow will be cast on the opposite side to the lantern.

Ideally, the actor should be lit from both sides and from the front, although this can be a very expensive use of lanterns.

The follow spot

The follow spot is a hard-edged spotlight that can be manoeuvred from the back of the auditorium to follow the actor's movement.

Uplighting

Lighting the actor from below can create a large shadow. This can help build up tension or create a melodramatic effect. It can be useful for the entrances of such characters as Dracula, Bill Sykes, a gunman, etc.

The control desk

Control desks vary from manual-operated through to computerised where the lighting cues can be preset.

A simple control desk may look like the one in the diagram below:

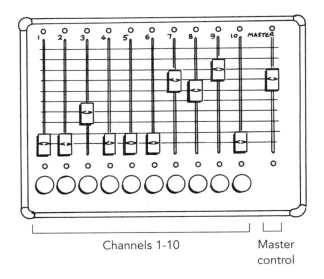

Channels 1-10   Master
                                        control

Channels 1-10 operate the lanterns. The closer the sliding switch is to the numbers at the top, the stronger the light. If the switch is at the bottom, then the lanterns linked to that channel will not be on. The master switch controls all of the channels. For example, if you set the sliding switches for channels 3, 7, 8 and 9, you can move the master switch up or down to control all these four channels at once.

Patching

A basic lighting set-up will consist of a patching board (also called a dimmer rack), a control desk and the lanterns. As you operate a channel on the control desk, this feeds into the patching board, which in turn feeds into the lantern socket. Most drama studios have a number of patching boards, but in order to explain we shall consider a simplistic set-up.

In the diagram shown on page 23, the patching board has six channels with two sockets per channel.

Generally, there will be an on/off switch and perhaps a pre-heat switch. The pre-heat switch lets the equipment 'warm-up'; this helps prevent fuses blowing. There are two plugs for each patching channel. Each of the channels on the patching board has three fuses – a master fuse for each channel and two smaller fuses for each of the sockets. Sometimes, when you think a bulb in the lantern has blown, it can be that a fuse on the patching board needs replacing. Fuses should be replaced by a technician.

Each of the channels in the control desk is linked to two sockets on the patching board. These sockets are linked to two further sockets on the lighting bar where the lanterns plug in. If you switch plugs round on the patching board, then the channels on the control desk will control different combinations of paired lighting.

Consider the diagram. Channel 1 on the control desk is linked to channel 1 on the patching board. These are linked to the lanterns at A and B. By swapping the bottom plugs in channels 1 and 6 on the patching board, the slides on channel 1 of the control desk will work lanterns A and L. The slides on channel 6 will work lanterns B and K. It is best not to change plugs around when the patching board is switched on.

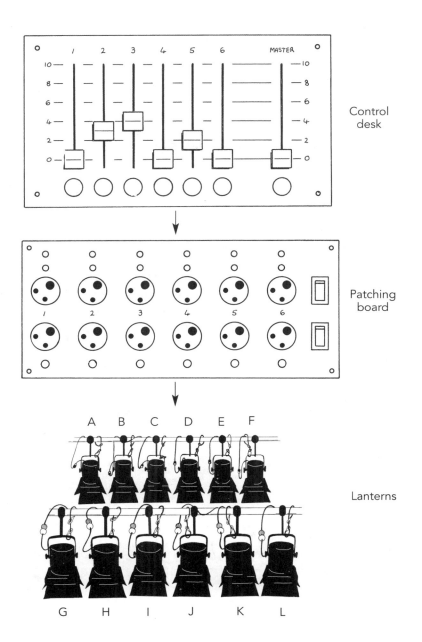

Control desk

Patching board

Lanterns

Some patching boards have an override switch for all or each of the channels. When this is pressed down, the lanterns will come on without using the control desk.

Always consult your teacher or a technician when organising lighting.

Planning the lighting for an improvisation/play

When planning the lighting for an improvisation or play, you should create:

- a ground plan with details of special lights
- a cue sheet.

Ground plan

Draw up a plan of the area to be used by the actors. There may be areas you want to light for effect but your main concern should be the actors. Watch rehearsals through so that you can see how much of the area the actors use. Your lights should be set so that the areas are covered and the special lights, eg particular spotlights, are aimed. The plan below shows the main acting area in sections (A-F) with special lighting requests marked with circles (X, Y, Z).

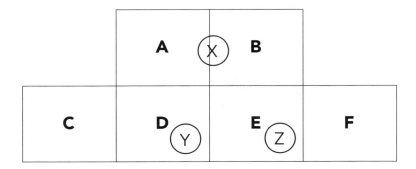

There will often be restrictions on the number of lights available. This could mean you will need to talk to the actors/director about the areas in which they stand. For example, if a solo singer begins their song in area C then, in order to pick up a spotlight, they need to move to area Y.

Cue sheet

After the ground plan, draw up a cue sheet. Cues should be listed in order. Next to each cue number should be the dialogue or action on which you change the lighting pattern. An example lighting cue sheet is provided below.

Cue number	Cue	Channel	Deck
Cue 1	Ruth: You'll never get it at that price.	5, 6, 7, 11	Upper
Cue 2	Exit of Pearl Minnie Edge	Snap blackout	Lower
Cue 3	Beryl: In that case, I'm off to the gym.	3, 2, 9, 18	Upper
Cue 4	Bryce: The deal has to be signed today.	Snap blackout	Lower

The first column in the example on page 25 is the cue number, the second column is the cue and the third and fourth columns are specific to the control desk you are using. The example cue sheet refers to an 18-channel desk with an upper and lower deck. This means that there can be up to 36 lanterns in use and that you can cross over from deck to deck as you meet cues. Hence, you can set the channels for cue 1 on the upper deck, the channels for cue 2 on the lower deck, and so on. For example, for cue 3 you would make sure that channels 3, 2, 9 and 18 are set on the upper deck so that, as you slide up the master switch or cross over on the cue of 'Beryl: In that case, I'm off to the gym', the lighting pattern changes.

With two decks you will always be ready for the next cue. The snap blackout referred to is an immediate blackout (see page 21). There is a snap blackout switch on most control desks. There are also usually timer controls which allow you to fade in and out. Many schools use computerised lighting desks which make the process less hectic as all plots can be preset. However, because the performance is live, you still need to be able to work the control desk in case any changes are necessary. Of course, with a computerised lighting desk you will still need a ground plan and a cue sheet, and the lanterns will need to be hung and positioned.

A blank lighting cue sheet is provided on page 27 for your use.

Lighting cue sheet

Production:

Cue number	Cue	Channel	Deck

Lighting worksheet

1   What is the difference between a profile and a fresnel spotlight?

....

....

2   What are the two main purposes of the lanterns?

....

....

3   What does 'finding your light' mean?

....

....

4   What are the houselights?

....

....

5   What is the function of a flood?

....

....

6   Why is a safety chain necessary?

....

....

7 What difference do barn doors make?

   ....

   ....

8 What is cinemoid used for?

   ....

   ....

9 What is a gobo?

   ....

   ....

10 Ideally, from how many sides should an actor be lit?

   ....

   ....

11 What is a follow spot?

   ....

   ....

12 What effect can you create by using uplighting?

   ....

   ....

2 Sound

"If music be the food of love, play on..."

(Twelfth Night)

Music

Music is very useful for creating atmosphere. Often, opening and closing the drama with music makes the work seem less ragged. Sometimes the lyric, tempo or style of the music may underline the theme of the dramatic piece. If music is needed as background, remember that the actors need to be heard and must be able to speak above it. If music is used in a public performance, then permission should be obtained from the Peforming Right Society Ltd.

Sound cues

Many sound effects can be found on CD or mini-disk. The most important factor with sound and music is that you must come in at the right time. For big productions, there will be at least one technical rehearsal. The director will run the production through from beginning to end, often missing out some of the dialogue so that the technical crew can make sure all sound and light cues work. For improvisations, knowing the script, having a list of sound cues and practising hitting the moment are essential. No matter how well you think you know the piece, concentration is essential.

Cues should be listed in order on a cue sheet. Next to each cue number should be the dialogue or action during which you produce the sound. An example sound cue sheet is provided below.

Cue number	Cue	Details	Duration
Cue 1	Tom: What time did you say they were arriving?	Car sound, track 2, effects CD 6	Fade out after thirty seconds
Cue 2	Sarah: And they left in a cloud of dust.	Prepared snippet of William Tell Overture	Twenty seconds

Equipment

Equipment could be as simple as a portable CD or mini-disk player. Often, schools have mixing desks. In some cases, the mixing desk plugs into an amplifier, but more often than not the amplifier is built into the desk. The desk or amplifier plugs into speakers. The desk gives you more precise control for fading in and out and can control CD players as well as microphones.

Microphones

There are various types of microphones. The more expensive the microphone, the better it is likely to be. Cheap microphones are trouble. They give poor sound quality and will cause feedback problems (see page 33). There are microphones with leads and radio microphones. Radio microphones do not have a lead, which puts fewer restrictions on the actor.

Radio microphones are expensive but most schools own one. In order to create a clear pick-up, the actor's mouth needs to be near the microphone. Alternatively, hanging several high-quality microphones over the acting area can pick up the actors' voices. For singing, actors are better using radio throat microphones. These are small microphones about 3 centimetres in length that are clipped to the costume near the throat. There is no lead. The microphone is picked up by a transmitter which plugs into the mains and the control desk.

If an actor/singer is using a hand-held microphone, it is wise to use a sponge cover over the part of the microphone held nearest to the mouth. This helps with the quality of sound by removing the clicking sounds that are often emitted when we speak.

During a production, it is better if the microphones are controlled by a sound engineer. The sound engineer can then fade the microphones out when they are not in use.

Feedback

Feedback is a high-pitched sound created when the microphone is directly in front of a speaker. Avoid this problem by setting the speakers from the public address system as far downstage as possible.

Foldback

The sound from the speakers is usually directed at the audience and away from the actor/singer. Foldback speakers are additional speakers which allow the musician/actor/singer to hear their voice and the accompaniment. These speakers are pointed towards the performer, not in the direction of the audience. The foldback can be adjusted on the control desk so that certain sounds are more prominent than others. For example, the singer may want the keyboards to be the loudest.

Foldback speakers

Sound control desk

The diagram below is a simple version of a sound control desk with eight channels. This means that up to eight individual instruments, microphones, etc can be used. The main controls have been identified and are explained.

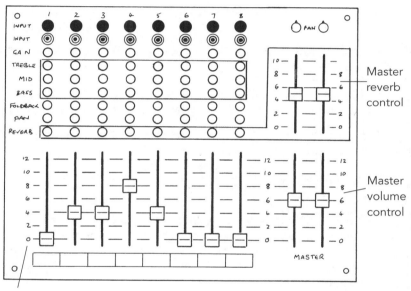

Master reverb control

Master volume control

Sliding volume control

Individual inputs – This is where the output lead from the microphone, musical instrument or music centre is placed. There is generally a choice of two input sockets – one for a jackplug and one for a three-pronged lead input. Whichever type of output lead you use, always make sure that it is plugged in firmly.

Gain – This controls the volume of the channel and the individual instrument or microphone.

Sliding volume control (individual) – This gives more precise volume control.

Master volume control – This controls all the channels together so that the volume can be adjusted to suit the venue. The two slide controls are for the left and right speakers.

Reverb – This helps create a fuller sound by adding a slight echo effect.

Master reverb control – This gives a general control over all the reverb being used.

Treble – This is a tone adjuster to help create more treble. However, too much treble can create feedback problems.

Mid – This provides tone control to create a little more treble and make the sound clearer and natural.

Bass – This provides tone control to give more bass and depth to the sound.

Foldback – Often, a foldback speaker is added to the sound system and directed at the musicians so that they can hear particular instruments or the general sound (see page 34). The foldback control on each of the channels allows you to decide what you want to hear. For example, if you only want to hear one instrument, the foldback from all the other channels can be switched off.

Pan – By turning this control to the left or right, the sound will come out of the appropriate speaker. This can be useful to suggest that sound is moving from one area to another, for example, a departing car or motorbike. If the control is left in a central position, the sound comes out of both speakers.

Extras

Various other effects can be added by using chorus pedals, reverb units and digital reverb units. These can be plugged in to individual channels. Some systems allow an echo or reverb unit to be looped into the system. It is then available to all channels.

Most control desks have a built-in graphic equaliser allowing further manipulation of the tones. A separate graphic equaliser can be attached to the control desk to help combat feedback.

Below is a simplified diagram of the inputs and outputs of a control desk.

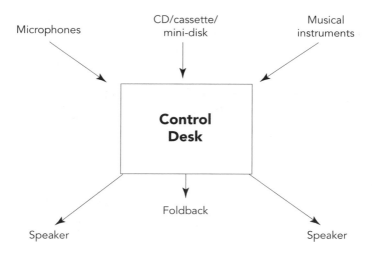

Other ways of creating sound

If you are putting together an improvisation, there are a number of interesting ways in which the actors can create sounds. There are a number of techniques you could use just with your voice, eg whispering, repetition of key words, overlapping of dialogue, etc. You can also create effects through clapping, clicking your fingers, rubbing your hands, etc.

The use of everyday objects or even the properties onstage can also be used effectively, for example, rubbing your finger on the rim of a glass until a high-pitched whine is created. This idea will be familiar to most people. When linked with other sounds, it becomes very effective and can underline the tension of a piece. Other ideas might be the clinking together of metal goblets to symbolise a clock striking, the tapping of the staging to create drum effects, crinkling various types of paper to suggest weather conditions. A lot of the sound effects recorded on CD and mini-disk are created with the simplest of objects. You can create an interesting collage of sound by recording one word or a short sentence that a character might say, recording further words or sentences and playing this back using a reverb unit. This effect can be useful in dream sequences or abstract pieces.

If you prepare a tape or disc of sound effects for your improvisation or production, make sure you make a back-up copy.

It's also great fun to work with live musicians.

Sound cue sheet

Production:

Cue number	Cue	Details	Duration

Sound worksheet

1 What is 'feedback'?

   ....

   ....

2 What difference does reverb make?

   ....

   ....

3 What is the advantage of using a radio microphone?

   ....

   ....

4 What is the function of the foldback speaker?

   ....

   ....

5 What does it mean to 'pan' the sound?

   ....

   ....

6 Describe three ways in which you could create sound effects.

   a ....

      ....

   b ....

      ....

   c ....

      ....

3 Costumes

"Give me my robe, put on my crown..."

(Antony and Cleopatra)

Styles of costumes

Styles of costume can go from the absolutely stunning through to the simple and practical but effective. Let us consider an abstract piece of drama which involves six students all playing a variety of roles. Students involved in creating an examination piece for drama will often devise something on these lines. As the students constantly change roles, they may decide it is a good idea to dress everyone in black and maybe use a few token costumes, eg a hat, a crown, a cloak, etc to indicate the different roles. This notion of costume is certainly simple and effective. However, one drawback is, if the piece is presented to an examiner for marking, he/she may have difficulty working out who is playing which role. The more time an examiner spends trying to work out who is doing what, the less time he/she spends on awarding marks for the drama work they are seeing. If you stick with the idea of black, then you would need to think of ways of easily identifying yourself for examination purposes, eg you could add different-coloured wristbands or headbands. Another variation on the simple costume is that each member of the group could wear a different colour. The colours could even be symbolic in relation to their character.

For more elaborate costumes, then the following should be considered:

- Responsibility

- Time and cost

- Colour in relation to the set

- Comfort and durability

- Period.

Responsibility

In large-scale productions, a wardrobe supervisor is essential. They will organise the buying in, hiring and making of costumes. They will take responsibility for the costumes during the production run and afterwards.

They will oversee the costumes during the performances, collect the costumes at the end of a performance, see to any cleaning or repairs and make sure they are in place for the next performance.

Professional and amateur companies may have a range of costumes and are generally prepared to lend or hire them out. For schools, storage can be a problem. Most schools tend, therefore, only to keep one or two of their own costumes.

In small improvisations, perhaps each student can look after their own costume. In bigger productions, it is helpful for each member of the cast to provide a coat hanger with a label identifying their name and the character they play. Looking after costumes during a school production can be a nightmare. If you are involved as an actor, try to be as helpful as possible. There are some tips to remember on page 44.

- Turn up on time for any fittings.

- Look after your costume.

- Report any tears or grubbiness.

- Make sure you know where your costume is prior to a performance.

- Make sure you return the costume to whoever is in charge of wardrobe after each performance.

- Try to assist in the making of the costume or collecting appropriate items if possible.

- Provide and hang your costume on a coat hanger that is labelled with your name and your character's name.

Time and cost

Even in the professional theatre, cost is very much an issue. The wardrobe department is given a budget and is expected to work within it. The wardrobe supervisor must also consider the time it takes to create costumes and when they have to be ready. Making the costumes can be fun and often parents will help, but some special costumes may need to be hired or bought in order to save time. In a production like *Oh What a Lovely War*, to create a lot of different costumes as well as the Pierrot costumes can be expensive. Sometimes a more simplistic approach, for example, dressing the cast in black trousers and T-shirts with the motif of a poppy can be cheaper and just as effective. For an examination, a candidate may have several months to create a costume.

Colour in relation to the set

It is important to get the right balance. You do not want the costume colours clashing with the set colours, but at the same time you do not want them so alike in colour to the set that the actor disappears onstage. Costumes are part of the visual spectacle of theatre and careful thought should be given to colours.

White costumes can look very effective against a black background, but if the actors are rolling on the floor or doing a lot of kneeling, the white costume will soon become very grubby, even during the performance. The colour of the costumes, like the set, can be symbolic or themed. For example, all the costumes can be a combination of blue, red and white to represent the three colours of the American flag.

Comfort and durability

Tight-fitting costumes restrict the actor's movement and so could affect their movement in relation to the character. If the costume is uncomfortable, this can cause the actor to fidget. The costume will become hot under the lanterns so wearing heavy coats can make you perspire and affect your concentration. Beware of using some materials such as plastic. Adapting a black binliner is generally not a good idea; it will rustle and spoil the overall effect. It will force the actor to keep unnecessarily still in order to reduce the noise from the costume.

The costume may have to be used for five or more performances so the strength of the material is important. You should also consider how the costume will be treated during the performance. For instance, is anyone pulled by the collar, or is a coat dragged off? The costume may have to withstand this treatment during a run of performances and don't forget the dress rehearsals.

Period

Be aware of the time when the play is set. Do some research on the period. Try to get photographs or pictures of how people dressed during the time. Trainers are OK but only in the appropriate time – if your drama is set in 1900, then trainers are not appropriate! As an actor, think of how you look. Check to see if you are wearing inappropriate jewellery, watches, etc. You may even wish to consider how appropriate your hairstyle is.

Other points

Characterisation

The costume should tell us about the character, eg the Pink Ladies wear pink tops and the T-Birds wear leather jackets. These costumes define their gangs.

Lanterns

Bear in mind the effect the lanterns will have on the costume:

- Many costumes become transparent under the lights.
- Insipid colours tend to disappear.

Footwear

Be very careful how you choose footwear for a performance. There is nothing worse than the noise from heavy, high-heeled shoes drowning out the dialogue.

Modern dress

It can be popular to do 'modern dress' productions. Some small educational theatre groups argue that modern-day dress versions of Shakespeare help the students to identify with the characters.

Hats

Hats can be a useful addition to a costume but can cause a few problems:

- They can be knocked off as you enter through a doorway.
- They can fall off because of sudden movement.
- They can cast a shadow over the eyes.
- Badly-fitting hats look comical and can spoil the seriousness of the character.

Organising yourself

If you are involved in a large-scale production make a careful note of:

- meetings to discuss the costume
- fittings
- dress rehearsals.

There is an example costume information sheet on page 48 and a blank sheet on page 49.

Costume sheet – example

Name: Jennifer Ruth Walker

Character name: Grace Beverly Bryce

Production: The Normalising Machine

Meetings to discuss costume

September 19th, 4.30 pm

October 2nd, 4.30 pm

Fittings

October 8th, 4.00 pm

October 16th, 4.00 pm

October 21st, 4.00 pm

Costume details: Black trousers, silver top, white shoes

Dress rehearsals: October 23rd, 2.00 pm, October 24th, 4.00 pm

Production dates: October 25-27th

Costume sheet

Name: ....

Character name: ....

Production: ....

Meetings to discuss costume

Fittings

Costume details:...

....

Dress rehearsals: ....

....

Production dates: ....

....

Costume worksheet

1   What is the job of a wardrobe supervisor?

   ....

   ....

2   How can lanterns affect costumes onstage?

   a ....

   b ....

3   Why does costume material need to be strong?

   ....

   ....

4   What are some of the problems that can be caused by wearing a hat onstage?

   ....

   ....

5   What is important about choosing footwear for a production?

   ....

   ....

6   During a production run, you should provide a coat hanger and a label for your costume. What should you write on the label?

   ....

   ....

4 Properties

"Is this a dagger which I see before me...?"

(Macbeth)

Stage and personal properties

Properties are items that can be either added to the set or carried on by an actor. Some of them will be functional, for example, a kettle that boils, a lamp that lights, a torch, etc. Properties placed in the acting area, for example, a vase of flowers, are stage properties. Properties carried on by the actor, for example, a comb or a newspaper, are personal properties. In a production there will be a property supervisor. He/she collects all necessary properties, checks they are in place before the production, supervises the construction of any special properties, collects them up after the production and either stores or returns them at the end of the production run. When you are acting in a large-scale production or an improvisation, always check your properties are in place before the performance. The property supervisor will do this as well but it is a good idea for you to double check. Complete a personal properties sheet – you will find it helpful. There is an example on page 54 and a blank sheet on page 55. The stage manager will also find this sheet useful.

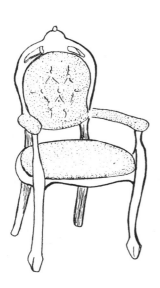

The property supervisor should make a list of properties required for the production and notes to help him/her obtain them. An example is provided on page 56 and a blank sheet on page 57.

The property supervisor will also need to make lists of properties on and offstage. Properties for onstage are properties for the acting area. Properties for offstage are properties for the sides or wings of the acting areas. Properties to be picked up by the actors are often placed on tables in the wings. See pages 58 and 59 for blank lists. The director and actors should always consider which properties are necessary. Whatever is taken onstage often has to be taken off. This can slow up the pace of a production. The more properties you use, the more you have to remember. Sometimes you can mime using a particular article – this can add another interesting dimension to your work. If you do use mime, be precise and practise the routine just as you would if you were using a property.

There is a tradition in professional theatre never to use real flowers or plants. The main reasons are:

- an actor may be allergic to them and could sneeze during a performance

- under hot lights, real flowers will fade and wilt quickly

- artificial flowers and plants are lighter to carry around

- imitation plants can be used again in another production.

Like costumes, durability is a factor. Again, colour is also important if you want them seen. A property painted black will disappear against a backdrop of a black drape – ask a magician!

Properties need to be appropriate to the time in which the drama is set. Properties help give the audience information about the period. For example, make sure the telephones you are using are from the right period, make sure modern wristwatches, etc are removed if not appropriate.

Properties can also be used to make statements about the content of the drama. For example, if the drama is about someone who continually reads the same book, the book could become bigger in each scene to symbolise the book dominating that person's life.

If possible, duplicate properties just in case of accidents or accidental loss, and always rehearse with the properties so you are familiar with the routines.

Personal properties sheet – Example

Name: Andrew Bede

Character name: Ben Percent

Production: The Normalising Machine

Property	Act	Page	Positioned
Contracts	1	12	Offstage left
Cup	1	18	Offstage right
Wallet	1	24	Jacket pocket
Contract Pen	1	25	Offstage left Jacket pocket
Trophy	2	30	Offstage left
Gun	2	35	Offstage right

Personal properties sheet

Name: ....

Character name: ....

Production: ....

Property	Act	Page	Positioned

Properties sheet – Example

Production: Sandgran

Properties needed	Possible source	Obtained?
Three buckets and spades	Advertise on staff noticeboard	
Handbag	Ask Grandma	
Newspapers	Collect seven	
Comb		✔

Properties sheet

Production:

Properties needed	Possible source	Obtained

Properties sheet – Onstage

Production:

Properties	Stage area	Act	Notes

Properties sheet – Offstage

Production:

Properties	Personal?	Stage left?	Stage right?	Notes

Properties worksheet

1   Why should you not use real flowers or plants during
    a production?

    ....

    ....

2   Give an example of a personal property.

    ....

    ....

3   Give an example of a stage property.

    ....

    ....

4   Why should you duplicate properties?

    ....

    ....

5   Why do you think you should rehearse with properties?

    ....

    ....

5 Set design

"What country, friends, is this?"

(Twelfth Night)

In the professional theatre, the set designer works very closely with the director as they interpret the play. The set will contribute to:

- the period
- defining place
- restricting or creating opportunities for movement
- restricting view
- creating levels
- the symbolism of the piece.

Rostra and levels

When you visit many professional companies, you can come away thinking that their sets would be difficult to emulate. In some ways, it is a good idea not to try but to go for minimalist sets instead. By simply using rostra, you can create an interesting set.

There are a number of companies who make interlocking staging rostra that you can construct to create all sorts of levels.

You can use a cyclorama (see page 15) to symbolise place. For example, lighting it with green could represent the countryside.

Consider such items as chairs. Are they really necessary? Once they are on the set, they will probably have to remain there. Using rostra means you have more flexibility. Rostra are not as dangerous to stand on as chairs. One of the most irritating effects of using chairs is the scraping of the legs against the floor. If it is really necessary to bring on a chair, then lift it carefully.

The box set

The box set is like a room or part of a room. The sides and back are generally constructed with flats. These are wooden frames with canvas stretched across them. The canvas can be painted.

Several flats can be joined together to create the box set. They are usually about 250 centimetres in height. The set can be simple (see the picture on page 14) or elaborate with functional doors, windows, lights, etc.

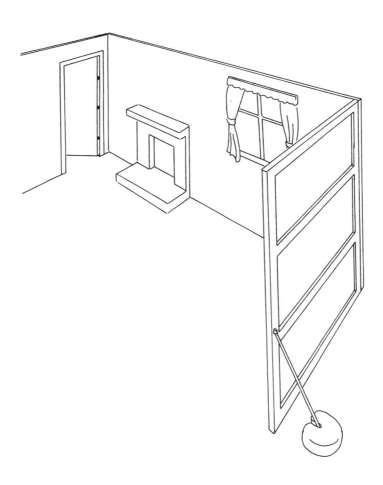

Swivel sets

Small box sets can be constructed so that they are reversible. A swivel set can save you time in scene changeovers.

Fixed sets

Box sets can be fixed, or can have castors so that they can be wheeled on and off. In most professional theatres, sets are moved on and off by tracks fastened to the stage or by flying in the scenery.

If the set is to be fixed, it will be necessary to measure the staging area and mark out where the flats, etc will be fixed. Create a scale drawing first. You should also think about constructing a model of the set. A set designer in the professional theatre will always construct a model so that he/she can discuss it with the director.

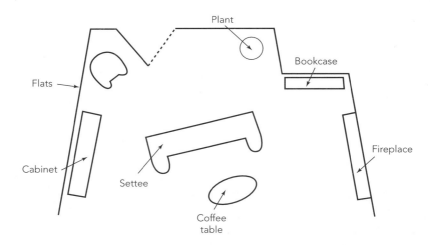

Sightlines

Don't forget to take into account the audience sightlines, ie the areas of the stage the audience can see.

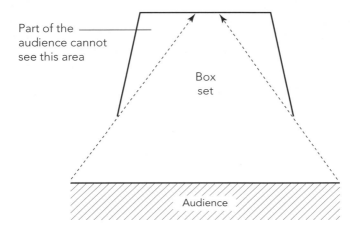

Dotted lines represent sightlines

If actors are entering from the wings (the sides of the stage), check when an actor is out of sight and mark a line that they should not step over when offstage.

Stage areas

To help with communication between those involved in a production, it is useful to know the names of the areas of the stage. Some people refer to six areas, others nine and some even more. The diagrams below show the breakdown into six and nine areas.

Upstage right	Upstage centre	Upstage left
Downstage right	Downstage centre	Downstage left

Audience

Upstage right	Upstage centre	Upstage left
Centre stage right	Centre stage	Centre stage left
Downstage right	Downstage centre	Downstage left

Audience

Style of staging

There are five main ways of staging a performance:

- End on
- Thrust
- Traverse
- In the round
- Promenade.

End on – The audience is directly in front of the acting area.

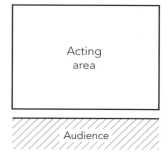

Thrust – The audience is on three sides of the acting area.

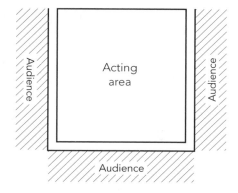

Traverse – The audience is on both sides of the acting area.

In the round – The audience is all around the acting area.

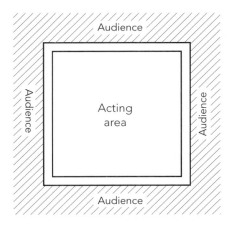

Promenade – The audience follows the actors from area to area. This style is often popular with outdoor productions in public parks, etc.

Set design worksheet

1   What are 'flats'?

....

....

2   What are 'sightlines'?

....

....

3   Name six areas of the stage.

a ....

b ....

c ....

d ....

e ....

f ....

4   Where is the audience sitting in relation to an 'end on'
    performance?

....

....

5   Describe 'promenade' theatre.

....

....

6 Stage management

"The play's the thing..."

(Hamlet)

Stage manager's job

In the professional theatre, the director of the performance will consult with a designer (or designers) about the set, lighting and sound. Once the process of constructing the set has begun, the stage manager oversees the progress, reporting to the director and designer as necessary. The stage manager is very much hands-on, with responsibility for carpenters, electricians, painters, etc.

"Has anyone seen the stage manager?"

However, the stage manager's job is bigger than this. As well as preparing for the show, he/she is very much the main person during the running of the show. The director decides how the show will be presented but the stage manager makes sure the mechanics of the production happen.

The stage manager oversees:

- set construction/striking the set
- costumes and properties
- communication
- organising play copies
- assistant stage manager/crew/runners
- the prompter.

As it is impossible to be in more than one place at once, fortunately most stage managers have one or more assistants (assistant stage managers, or ASMs) and hopefully a stage crew to help with the night-to-night running of a production. The most important personality trait is to be able to remain calm under stress. If anything goes wrong – and it often does – panic will only make things worse. No matter who is frantic around him or her, the stage manager must remain calm.

The stage manager should take early opportunities to view rehearsals and make notes of exits and entrances and any particular stage business. During final rehearsals and the production run, the stage manager will be backstage. He or she does not see the final show from the auditorium. However, in a school production or small workshop, it is possible to have a team supporting the stage manager who can run the backstage work for one night allowing the stage manager to enjoy watching a finished performance.

If you are acting as stage manager and a teacher is the director, then they will give precise instructions as to what your job entails.

A blank production sheet is provided on page 81 so that the names of those in charge of various elements of the production can be noted.

Set construction/striking the set

Set construction can take quite some time. In professional theatre, the stage manager would have the assistance of carpenters and electricians. In a school production, a lot of the assistance in set building, etc is given with goodwill. Try to organise as many things as early as possible. People who are not directly involved will not be aware of all your different deadlines and won't realise how much has to come together at the end. If someone offers to construct the basic set then give them a deadline. You will probably have to paint and dress the set and this all takes time. (Dressing the set means adding the bits and pieces which enhance the look, for example, a bowl of flowers, shrubbery, etc.)

At the end of the production run, the stage manager organises the dismantling of the set. This is called 'striking the set'. In professional theatre, this takes place almost immediately after the production is over so that work on the set for the next production can begin.

In a small improvisation, this might be as simple as putting away a few chairs and rostra, but it is a job that needs doing. All areas should be left tidy.

Costumes and properties

Generally, someone will take particular responsibility for properties and costumes. However, the stage manager will have to make sure that the properties are in place. Make a list of all properties. (See the sheets on pages 54 to 59.) Note where properties should be placed. At the end of each performance, collect them all in, and store them somewhere safe ready for the next performance.

Properties are divided into stage properties and personal properties. Stage properties go in the acting area; personal properties are carried by the actors, eg a briefcase, a letter. Each actor should check his/her personal properties but it is also always useful if the stage manager checks as well.

Some costumes and properties will be bought, but often items are borrowed. Look carefully after anything borrowed and return it at the end of the production run. Try not to borrow items that could be broken.

Communication

The responsibility to post up rehearsal schedules lies with the stage manager, although in a school production this may be organised by the director. There should be at least one technical rehearsal when lights, sounds, special effects, etc are tried. It is important that the stage manager is present to coordinate and make notes of any problems or adjustments that are needed.

The stage manager will give the cues for everyone to begin the performance. Often in a school production, a member of staff may greet the audience and inform them of fire doors, toilets, refreshments, etc. As this person finishes their speech, this could be the cue for the houselights to be taken down. The stage manager may wish to control the houselights. Don't forget the houselights need to be switched on at the end of the first act for the interval and at the end of the performance.

If you feel the sound is too loud or quiet, mention it to the sound engineer during the interval.

Organising play copies

All actors and those assisting with the play will need accurate scripts. The director in a school production may organise this but certainly the stage manager should mark up the copies to be used backstage during the production run. The following should be noted:

- all exits and entrances
- when the actors should be called (always call the actors in good time)
- any properties to be taken onstage
- a check of any personal properties
- cues for the houselights.

Assistant stage manager/crew/runners

The assistant stage manager will work specifically under the stage manager and will help to ensure all jobs are organised and taking place.

Runners should be on hand to deliver any messages between sound and light crews and backstage. They will also be sent by the stage manager to call the actors to their places prior to their entrances. Offstage actors should wait in a central place or their dressing rooms and be ready for their call. Prior to the show commencing, the stage manager will alert all crew and actors at five minutes to countdown. This is referred to as 'beginners'.

Make sure everyone knows his or her job. Some jobs may be as simple as mopping the set down before the production, but you need to make sure this is done in good time so that it can dry before the performance. Backstage noise can spoil a performance, so ensure that there is quiet at all times. If stage crew need to move scenery during the performance, they should wear black and should do the job as quickly and quietly as possible. It is also a good idea if the backstage crew wear shoes that will not squeak or make unnecessary noise.

The prompter

The prompter is responsible to the stage manager. Again, this is a job that needs someone who will remain calm in a crisis. A prompter should be confident and not afraid to give a line if he or she thinks an actor has forgotten it. The prompter should sit in a place where the actors can see him or her. If an actor forgets their line, he or she should look at the prompter and say the word 'Yes'. The prompter should then return the line. The prompter should attend a number of the rehearsals in the final stages. Actors may still be unsure of their lines and a prompt will help the rehearsals run smoothly. The prompter should note when there are dramatic pauses or no dialogue because of movement. Most importantly, the prompter's script should be up-to-date.

"Erm... Yes"
"When shall we three meet again?"

Production sheet

Production:
Performance:
Stage:
Assistant stage manager:
Runners:
Properties:
Costumes:
Set design:
Set construction:
Lighting engineer:
Lighting assistant:
Sound engineer:
Sound assistant:
Prompter:
House management:
Refreshments:

Stage management worksheet

1   What is 'striking the set'?

....

....

2   What is an ASM?

....

....

3   What should the stage manager note on the copy of the play
    for backstage?

....

....

....

....

....

4   What does 'beginners' mean?

....

....

5   What is the job of the prompter?

....

....

7 Performance tips

"Play out the play."

(Henry IV, Part 1)

In position

Be in position early. It is unfair if anyone has to try and find you. In big productions, it is probable that the director will want to speak to all the cast about 15 minutes before the performance commences. You will probably be warned about 'beginners' by the stage manager. Beginners means you should be in place ready to start. There is no time to go to the toilet now! If you come offstage during the performance, make sure you go to the place you have been told to go. Make sure you know when your next entrance is – be ready, be early. It is better to make an entrance early than late as this affects the pace of a play.

If you are presenting an improvisation for another class or an examiner, you may need to be ready in the acting area. If this is the case, create a good impression by being still and calm. This will help you with your concentration. An examiner will always look at how you are positioned before the drama begins. It sends out signals to him or her. Make sure you send the right signals.

Fidgeting

Try not to:

- flick your hair
- scratch
- rock on your feet
- keep turning round when facing out of the drama.

If it really becomes necessary to flick your hair out of your eyes, then try to do it in character. Then sort your hair so it is not necessary in the next performance.

Acknowledging others in the acting area

When you pass another character in the acting area during a performance, consider how you should react as you pass them. Does your character know them? Do you nod, smile, ignore them, etc?

Mistakes

If you make a mistake, don't laugh – that will make two mistakes! Try to continue as if nothing has gone wrong. It is probable that the audience will not know the script and they certainly won't know an improvisation that you have created. During a large-scale production there is generally someone who will prompt. The procedure here if you forget your lines is to look at the prompter, say 'Yes' in character, hear the prompt, then repeat the line. The main rule when mistakes occur is to remain calm and draw as little attention to the problem as possible.

The performance run

Points to consider:

First night – There will be a lot of excitement and concentration is extremely important.

Second performance – Think about how well you and the cast performed. What can you improve?

Subsequent performances – Each performance will reveal something that went better than previous performances and something that will need to be improved. It is probable that the director will draw the cast's attention to some of these points but you need to consider the good and poor parts of your own performance.

The last performance – It is your last performance, but for the audience it is their first performance. Don't be overconfident, and don't engage in any silly tricks or make any changes. Ad libs rarely work. You might know what you are going to do for an ad lib but others may not know how to react.

Generally, by the time you get to the last performance, you will be tired but your enjoyment of the whole run will create enough momentum to carry you through. Remember, it is the last time you will ever perform the play so make it a good one.

Saying thank you

It will be obvious that there will be key people to thank such as the director, lighting engineer, stage manager, etc but remember that, in a large-scale production, there are many other people involved. There is a thank you list on page 96 to help you.

In some school performances, at the end of the last show the cast call the director and main helpers onstage so that they can make a public thank you. The idea of the thank you is worthy but finishing this way can take away from the professionalism of the production run. It is better if the thank yous are made offstage, maybe half an hour before the final performance.

Blocking in

"and you on that mark"

This is the position someone takes in relation to the acting area and the audience. The blocking in is to allow for sightlines, ie characters are placed on the stage/acting area so that the audience can see them clearly. When presenting improvisations, always try to block in the actors downstage. It makes it easier for the audience to see and hear.

In the first picture of Goldilocks and the three bears, above, notice how the bed is downstage centre and the bears are facing out to the audience. Everyone can be seen clearly. In the second picture, below, the blocking in is very poor as we cannot see Goldilocks and the bears have their backs to the audience.

The use of the downstage area is very important. Consider key moments in an improvisation. Would you block them upstage or downstage? Using a small downstage area for the whole improvisation can create some interesting visual work. If you just use an area four metres by four metres, you are forced to use other techniques to create interesting visual images. For example, instead of exiting, the characters could just face out of the drama or hold a freeze-frame. This creates interesting drama and gives you the opportunity to show your understanding of various drama techniques.

The director can block the actors in for symbolism as well as sightlines. For example, the king can be blocked in on a high level to represent his power and the servant could be placed on a lower level to show that he is under the king's power. Imagine that in the story the king does a number of silly things and loses his throne, and the servant does some clever things and gains power. Their original blocking in positions can be reversed. Again, the visual image is symbolic and confirms details of the story for the audience.

Creating interesting pictures for the audience is important. The play is not a radio play but a play with words and visual action. In cinema, the director will be at pains to ensure that what we see is pleasing, atmospheric and appropriate.

Most people will be aware that the actor should not speak with their back to the audience, although occasionally breaking this 'rule' can create a dramatic effect. However, the majority of the time it is easier for the audience if they can see the actor clearly. Whenever possible, try to face the audience, keeping your shoulders towards them.

If you are speaking to someone onstage then you don't always need to look directly at them. Try to create angles as in the picture below so that part of your face is looking at the audience. You could always experiment with different positions. A person does not always need to face the person they are talking to. Both could face the audience directly.

If you are using chairs, then set them at 45 degrees – again, this makes it easier for the audience to see.

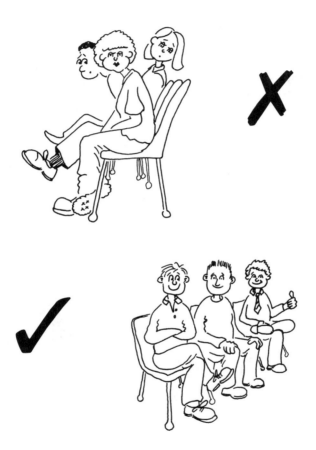

Using upstage hand

Also consider the use of hands across the face. In the first picture below, actor A calls to actor B but covers his face with his downstage hand. This can muffle the sound of the voice and hides the facial expression from the audience.

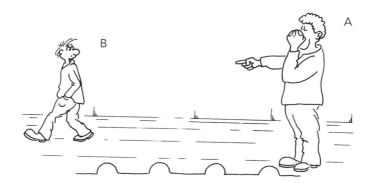

In this picture, actor A uses his upstage hand which makes everything clearer.

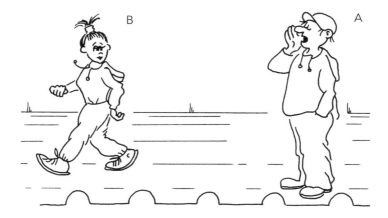

Blocking in for the round

The notes on blocking in so far have been relevant to end on performance – that is where the audience is directly in front of the actors. In theatre in the round, the audience is positioned all around the acting area and blocking in for sightlines needs much more thought. Consider the two diagrams below. In the first diagram, below, actors A and B are very close together. This obscures part of the view for the audience.

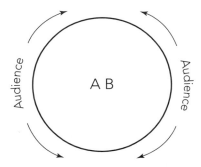

In the second diagram, below, there is a bigger gap between actors A and B, making it easier for the audience to see the actors.

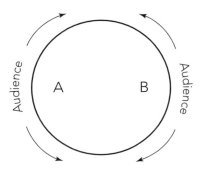

There are problems with the directions that actors A and B face in the diagrams below. A lot of the audience will just see actors' backs. When possible, have the actors facing different directions. In the round, try to give movements to the actors so that they move round the acting area so that different parts of the audience can see the actor's face. Of course, the trick is to make the movements purposeful. If an actor is moving only to find a different place in the acting area so that the audience can see, it will look obvious.

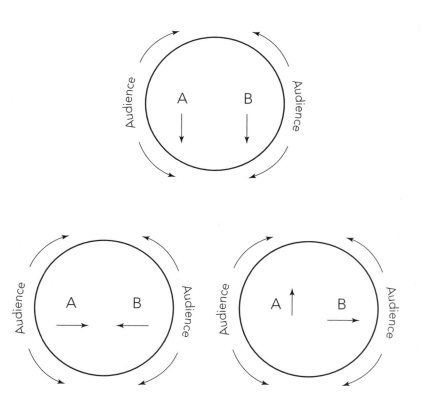

Telephone conversations

In simple presentation work for an audience, always think about the visual image you are making. Drama improvisations such as telephone calls can always be done in a more creative way than both actors cupping their hands to their faces and speaking back to back. Use abstract form to create an interesting picture.

Consider:

- side by side
- kneeling and facing each other
- sitting back to back
- one standing, one sitting
- side by side with arms extended to touch each other (to symbolise the connection).

Thank you list

- Director
- Musical director
- Producer
- Sound engineer/assistants
- Property supervisor
- Stage crew
- Runners
- Programme, tickets, poster designers
- Reprographics
- Publicity
- Refreshments
- House management
- Programme sellers
- Ushers
- Car park attendants
- Photographer
- Video recorder
- Carpenter
- Electrician

- Assistant directors
- Musicians
- Lighting engineer/assistants
- Costume supervisor
- Stage management
- Prompter
- Box office

There will probably be others. Find out who they are. One thank you will be appreciated.

8 Drama skills and techniques

"All the world's a stage..."

(As You Like It)

Giving witness/making point of view

"… and it had a round, roly thing at each corner!"

In role, you describe some event you have witnessed, giving the details from your point of view.

For example, you may have witnessed a robbery, an accident or a parade. This is a useful technique to use in historical dramas, eg you could describe the time you saw the first car, a public hanging, a workhouse or a coronation.

Secret role-play

Also called hidden role-play and special information. The teacher gives information to some students but not others.

For example, in pair role-play, the teacher may say to one student that they have been in trouble for stealing. Acting as a parent or guardian in the role-play, the partner attempts to find out information. In ensemble role-play, a student or a group of students are given special information. For example, as town planners they are presenting a project to the local community (the rest of the class in role). The teacher has given the town planners particular information about the project.

Bringing to life

In groups, students make a freeze-frame. The teacher tells you to bring the frame to life. The students role-play until the teacher calls "Freeze".

His/her thoughts

A person acts out a particular situation. Their partner or a small group relates the thoughts that person might be having.

For example, a mother is leaving a baby in a bus shelter. The partner relates the mother's thoughts to the audience during the action.

Sometimes the central person may not be involved in any direct action but may simply sit, stand or hold a freeze-frame. This technique is useful in prepared improvisations and will often be used by your teacher in improvisation work.

Good angel/bad angel

This technique is generally used in groups of three. To the left, one person plays the good angel, and to the right, another person plays the bad angel. The central character could be in some sort of dilemma; there is a decision to be made. Through the good and bad angels, they can consider different points of view.

For example, should he truant with his friends or go to school? The person playing the good angel gives reasons why he should not truant, and the person playing the bad angel gives reasons why he should truant. This is a useful technique to use with classroom/ studio work but can also be effective in prepared improvisations. For dramatic effect, more than one good and bad angel can be used.

Solo thinking

Students sit on the floor in a space by themselves. The teacher asks them to consider an issue or a particular role.

The teacher may give some ideas or key questions for the students to consider. After a while, the teacher may ask the students some direct questions or ask them to take on a role and share some of the thoughts the person might be having (thought in the head).

Sometimes after solo thinking, the teacher may suggest that each student makes a different statement about a character from the drama. These statements build up information on the character. Solo thinking is often used by the drama teacher at the end of a lesson so that the students are given the opportunity to consider the issues raised and the learning points of the session.

Amplifying

Sometimes called 'more and more'. The drama can be presented using abstract or realistic form. The dialogue/voice patterns begin very quiet and become louder and louder, or the actions begin very small and become bigger and bigger.

Of course, both the actions and the dialogue/voice patterns can increase at the same time.

Turning through the audience

When turning to face another actor in the acting area, try to make the turn bigger by turning through the longest way.

For example, actor A, who is facing upstage, has to turn to actor B:

Actor A   Actor B

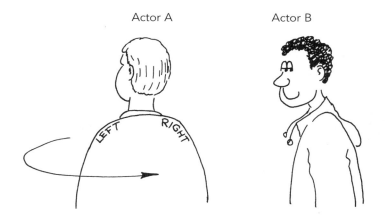

Actor A should turn through 270° by:

1 turning away from actor B so that his left shoulder is downstage
2 then facing directly downstage
3 turning to actor B so that his right shoulder is downstage.

The three stages are all one continuous action. It allows the audience to see more of the actor's face as he turns. This is useful if it is important for the audience to be aware of a character's thoughts as he/she turns.

Docudrama

Students present a piece of drama in the style of a television documentary.

The documentary may contain various interviews, action apparently caught on camera, re-enactments, reporters, link presenters, etc. It is often fun to present a docudrama of a character from literature, eg Macbeth. The docudrama could show interviews with the witches, Lady Macbeth or castle servants. Perhaps the police could be involved!

Split staging

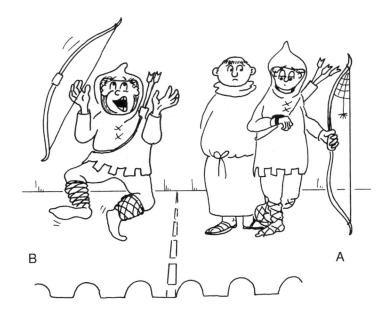

The acting area is split into two (sometimes more) areas.

In area A, the actors hold a freeze. The actors in area B present action from the drama. After a while, the actors in area B freeze and the actors in area A bring their drama to life. The action can move between area A and area B several times. The drama will look better if the freeze-frames are visually interesting.

Narrating

In the presentation of a drama piece, one or more persons speak directly to the audience, giving information and relating events of the story.

Often, the narrator will not be a character in the story. The narrative of the drama is the storyline.

9 Written work

*"Whate'er you think, good words,
I think, were best."*

(King John)

Writing a script

The way a script is set out is important. If you look at scripts in different books you will see that they can vary a little bit but they all more or less follow the same format:

1   The character's name is written first. It is followed by a colon (:).

    Peter:

2   The character's name is followed by the words he/she speaks.

    Peter: I'm going to buy that dog.

3   The next speaker begins on a new line.

    Peter: I'm going to buy that dog.
    Anne: Which one?

    Don't forget question marks or exclamation marks when necessary.

4   Stage directions indicate a reaction, movement or how something should be said. Put stage directions in brackets.

    Peter: (whispering) I'm going to buy that dog.
    Anne: (putting down the newspaper) Which one?

    If the stage directions are one word (whispering) or not a complete sentence (putting down the newspaper), you do not need to begin with a capital letter or finish with a full stop.

5   If the stage directions are a complete sentence, then a capital letter at the beginning and full stop at the end are necessary.

    Peter: (whispering) I'm going to buy that dog.
    Anne: Be careful, he might hear you. (She walks to the lounge door and looks into the hall.) He's coming!

Performing rights

Plays and musicals are protected by copyright. If a play is to be performed in public, then performance rights must be paid. This means that you pay the author and/or publisher a fee for each performance. Plays will have the details of the author and publisher in the front of the book. Performance rights should be obtained before you begin rehearsals.

"I said, CAN WE USE YOUR PLAY?"

A public performance becomes a public performance when at least one member of the public attends. Usually for performances in assemblies, lessons and examinations, it is not necessary to pay performing rights, however, it is always advisable to check. The cost of performing rights for a school performance is generally cheaper than for amateur or professional performances. The copyright owners may request that certain information is included in a certain size type on all posters and programmes. At the end of the production run, the box office will complete a form with similar information on it to the one on page 112.

Box Office Information

Production:

Date	Tickets sold	Complimentary tickets	Ticket price	Box office total

For the music score, there is generally a hiring fee payable in advance.

You will need to request the required number of scripts and scores as you will probably not be allowed to photocopy either the script or the score. If the script is to be altered in any way, then permission is needed from the copyright holder. The copyright of a play expires seventy years after the death of the author so, for example, the plays of William Shakespeare are copyright-free. It is the job of the director or producer to check the availability of the performing rights. Occasionally, performing rights will not be given if there is a professional production running in the West End or on tour.

Producing written work

In the *Student Handbook for Drama*, several pages were devoted to tips on producing written work for drama. The inclusion of examples of students' work was popular, so in this section I have included a few more.

The examples refer to:

- audience awareness
- symbolism
- body language
- involvement in the role-play.

Audience awareness

When you watch a production, look out for the ways in which the director has tried to ensure that the audience understands various points, does not miss out on important parts of the play and feels involved with the production. In the following example, Sarah was aware of the importance of the prologue in *Romeo and Juliet*:

> As the play started with the prologue, the man stood on a box so the audience's attention would be directed towards him. He spoke very loudly, slowly and very clearly. I think this made the audience realise that this part of the play needed to be listened to very carefully.

Laura identifies what happens when the actor in role sits with the audience:

> The actor playing Romeo sat in the audience and spoke his thoughts out aloud. This made the audience feel more involved because it was as if he was talking to us.

In the presentation of her improvisation about an abandoned baby, Katie is aware that the repetition of a word can make a point about the content to the audience:

> We used the word 'helpless' a lot as we thought it was important to let the audience know how weak the baby was, and how defenceless it was to the world.

In further work on the same theme, Sarah is aware of how silences and a carefully chosen sentence would help the audience think about the content. In this prepared improvisation, Sarah plays a young mother who is about to abandon her baby. She is accompanied by a friend:

> There was a lot of silence to show that it would be a really awkward situation to be in. It would create a tense atmosphere so that the audience would not know who was going to speak next.

> In my role I eventually knelt down and put the baby on the ground. We very slowly stood up to show how hard it was to say goodbye. My friend looked at the baby and then at me. I looked at the baby and said, 'I hope you can forgive me.' I think the simplicity of this line made the audience think about what was happening and would make them feel more involved.

> As we walked away from the bus stop, my friend turned her head and looked at the baby. We then froze, showing how much regret we had. We also thought that both the girls would want to have one last look at the baby and would want to keep the image in their heads. I think that this simple presentation was very effective because there was very little speaking throughout.

Getting physically close to the audience can force them to consider the issues of the drama. Sarah shows how her group developed the ending of another piece on the same theme to involve the audience:

> As the lines were said, the group moved closer to the audience so they would feel intimidated and would think about what we were saying. As the line 'All the strangers passing by' was said, the outer people crossed by each other and walked past the middle person. This not only symbolised what was being said, but also allowed some movement as we had stood still for a long time. To finish, we all said the last line 'Why?' together. This made it louder and would make the audience think about why someone would abandon a baby. We said the word forcefully and with full eye contact with the audience.

Symbolism

Debra notes how, in a production of *Macbeth*, the use of levels symbolised dominance:

> One of the actresses, who played a witch, stood on a higher level to show her dominance over Macbeth.

Emma describes how the use of a drumbeat in her improvisation symbolised the beating of the heart:

> The drum was tapped throughout and symbolised the heartbeat of us, the victims. Towards the end of the improvisation we all knelt on the floor and repeated the word 'die'. We whispered it. The drumbeat became quieter and quieter until it stopped. The stopping of the drumbeat symbolised our death. Our heads were down and the audience was silent.

Emma also shows how simple positioning in the acting area can be symbolic:

> The first part of the improvisation showed us standing in a line. This showed the audience that we were all equal – nobody had higher or lower status. Katie ran on and we began to circle her. Katie slowly curled herself up in a ball. This showed her as the victim and her fear.

When Laura watched *West Side Story*, she was aware of how space between Tony and Maria's hands in the dance routine symbolised that they should not be together:

> Tony and Maria came from opposite sides of the stage and met in the centre. They moved slowly, contrasting with the quick energetic dancers onstage. As they met, they began to dance, looking into each other's eyes, but the main symbolism was how they danced. When they put their hands towards each other, they did not make contact but always kept a small distance between them. To me, this symbolised that they were not allowed to be together and, as the story would show, they could never be together.

Body language

The body language in the last extract symbolises the future of the relationship between Maria and Tony. Body language gives us information. It tells us about people's moods, status and attitudes.

Sarah writes:

> I showed my disappointment by walking slowly with my head down.

When Leeanne watched *Macbeth*, she analysed his movement:

> To show that Macbeth was frightened of what he was being told, he walked backwards away from the witches. This showed he did not trust the witches.

When writing about her improvisation, Laura states:

> When I went in, I waited for them to tell me to sit down. This would indicate to the audience that I was trying to be polite. I sat down with my back straight, crossed my legs and put my hands on my knees to show I was trying to make a good impression.

In an improvisation, Laura refers to the body language but she also identifies how the turning away from her mother is symbolic:

> At the beginning of the improvisation I was sitting down, but as time progressed and the stress built up I stood up to show I was angry. I also put my hand on my head to show I was upset. I turned away from my mum to show I was upset with her.

Leeanne shows how her group use body language to show the audience the mood and attitude of a character:

> We performed an improvisation about a child who was bald and starting a new school. She was apprehensive about what other children would say. We decided that her body language would be defensive by wrapping her arms tightly around herself and putting her head down.

Clara is aware of how movement and body language underline statements her group wish to make:

> The way we acted towards each other changed between scenes a lot. When we were happy, we had contact with each other. We made sure we were all touching in some way. This showed that we were all working together and bonding. When we wanted to show that we had fallen out, we made sure there was no contact. Everyone stayed in their own space onstage.

Involvement in the role-play

In role-plays, students can become involved in the events, and the body language of others can send out signals that influence how someone will react in the drama.

John writes about being a manager in a role-play:

> In the role-play I was the new manager of the supermarket. Everyone had worked there for a long time and they had all hoped that Peter would be the new manager. I decided to have a meeting with the staff. I felt very nervous before addressing them. I gathered them around me but everyone gave me a cold look. The cold look made me realise that the meeting was going to be difficult.

David shows how use of a thought tunnel* gave him insight into a character and that he could use some of the information later:

> Jean had to walk through the thought tunnel and everyone had to call out how they thought Jean would be feeling as she walked to the social services. This gave us all a wider insight into her. Someone mentioned Jean's guilt. I hadn't thought that Jean could feel guilty so the thought tunnel made me think a bit more. It was also a good exercise for confidence and thinking quickly. During some pair work, I used the idea of guilt when I played Jean's father.

Kirsty comments on her involvement in the role-play, noticing how the teacher's role affects the atmosphere and how her own involvement forces actions from her:

> In the short role-play I played Isobella, William's wife. I visted him in gaol. Our teacher was in role as the gaoler walking round, repeatedly saying 'Only a few minutes left and remember there is to be no physical contact.' This created a tense and daunting atmosphere, just knowing there was only a short time to say goodbye to your husband before he was killed. You weren't allowed to kiss or hug him one last time.
>
> We sat facing each other and we both looked into each other's eyes. I felt extremely sad here. As the gaoler made his way round telling us it was time to go, we stood up and I said 'I love you'. As I walked slowly past him, I instinctively shut my eyes and inhaled deeply, as if to get one last smell of him.

* A definition of a thought tunnel is provided in the *Student Handbook for Drama*.

Useful words

This section lists words you will find useful when completing written work. You may also wish to add words of your own.

Abstract	Accompaniment	Acoustics
Acting area	Action	Actor
Actress	Amplifier	Amplifying
Angle	Assistant stage manager	Atmosphere
Audience	Auditorium	
Backcloth	Backstage	Barn door
Bass	Batten	Battery
Beginners	Blackout	Blocking in
Body language	Box office	Box set
Bringing to life	Budget	Bulb
Candle	Canvas	Carpenter
Cassette	Castors	CD
Centre	Changeover	Channel
Character	Choreographer	Chorus pedal
Cinemoid	Circle	Colour
Comfort	Communication	Concentration
Construction	Control desk	Copyright
Costume	Create	Crew
Cross over	Cue	Cut-out
Cyclorama		
Design	Dialogue	Digital
Dimmer	Director	Docudrama
Downstage	Drama	Dramatic
Drape	Dress rehearsal	Durability
Echo	Effect	Effective
Electrician	Electricity	End on
Engineer	Entrance	Equipment
Exit		
Fading	Feedback	Final

Finding your light
Fixed set
Flood
Foldback
Freeze-frame
Fuse

First night
Flash button
Flying in
Follow spot
Fresnel spotlight

Fitting
Flat
Focus
Footwear
Front of house

'G' clamp
Gobo
Ground plan

Gain
Good angel/bad angel

Giving witness
Graphic equaliser

His/her thoughts

Houselights

Image
Input

Improvisation
Instruments

In the round

Jackplug

Lanterns
Light
Lower deck

Lead
Lighting

Levels
Lighting bar

Make-up
Melodrama
Mime
Mixing desk
Music

Mask
Microphone
Mini-disk
Modern
Musical director

Master
Mid
Minimalist
Movement
Musician

Narrating

Narrator

Offstage
Output

Onstage

Operate

Pan
Performance
Permission
Playwright
Practising
Profile spotlight
Prompter
Public performance

Pantomime
Performing rights
Photographer
Plug
Presence
Programme
Properties
Publicity

Patching
Period
Picture
Point of view
Production
Promenade
Proscenium

Recording
Represent
Role
Rostrum
Run

Refreshments
Reprographics
Role-play
Round
Runner

Rehearsals
Reverb
Rostra
Royalty

Safety chain
Score
Set
Sightlines
Solo
Sound effects
Spotlight
Stage manager
Strobe lighting
Swivel set

Scene
Script
Set design
Snap blackout
Solo thinking
Speaker
Stage
Stage traffic
Supervision
Symbolic

Scenery
Secret role-play
Shadow
Socket
Sound
Split staging
Stage direction
Striking the set
Switch
Symbolise

Technical
Telephone
Theme
Ticket
Torch
Treble

Technician
Tension
Thought tunnel
Timer
Transmitter
Turning through the audience

Technique
Theatre in the round
Thrust
Tone
Traverse

Uplighting

Upper deck

Upstage

Visual

Wardrobe

Wings